AMERICA'S MOST WINNING TEAMS™

OHIO STATE FOOTBALL

ANN BYERS

rosen publishing's
rosen central®
New York

Published in 2014 by The Rosen Publishing Group, Inc.
29 East 21st Street, New York, NY 10010

First Edition

Library of Congress Cataloging-in-Publication Data

Byers, Ann.
Ohio State Football/Ann Byers.—First edition.
pages cm.—(America's most winning teams)
Includes bibliographical references and index.
ISBN 978-1-4488-9401-7 (library binding)—ISBN 978-1-4488-9438-3 (pbk.)—
ISBN 978-1-4488-9439-0 (6-pack)
1. Ohio State University—Football—History—Juvenile literature. 2. Ohio State Buckeyes (Football team—History—Juvenile literature. I. Title.
GV958.O35B94 2014
796.332'630977157—dc23
2012047049

Manufactured in the United States of America

CPSIA Compliance Information: Batch #S13YA: For further information, contact Rosen Publishing, New York, New York, at 1-800-237-9932.

CONTENTS

INTRODUCTION

No one expected the Buckeyes to win. Like the trees of western Ohio for which they were named, the Ohio State team was smaller than average. They had played in the Western Athletic Conference for only three years, and their record was less than impressive. Illinois, on the other hand, had been in the conference since the team was founded twenty years earlier. The Fighting Illini had been undefeated the last two years. The crowd in the stands was fully anticipating another Illinois triumph.

But the crowd had not yet seen Ohio's rookie halfback, Chic Harley. The sophomore could run, kick, pass, receive, and play defense. Despite his talents, however, Illinois dominated the game. With a minute and ten seconds left on the clock, the Buckeyes were behind 6–0. That's when Harley faked a pass, bolted past the Illini defenders, and tied the game with a touchdown. Then the multitalented halfback called a timeout, changed into dry shoes, and kicked the point after the touchdown. In the final seconds of the game, the relatively unknown Ohio Buckeyes defeated the two-time conference champions.

Harley's performance catapulted his team into the national spotlight. In that year, 1916, Ohio State enjoyed a perfect record—seven wins and no losses—and won its first Western Conference championship. The Buckeyes were finally in

In the final game of the 2012 season, Ohio State fans pour onto the field to celebrate their 26–21 win against their archrival, the University of Michigan.

"the big leagues"—a winning team. They would remain one of the most winning teams in college football for close to a hundred years. Ohio State has won seven national titles and been conference champion thirty-four times. Seven Ohio State players have received the Heisman Trophy, and seventy-eight have been named consensus all-Americans. Thirty players or coaches have been inducted into the College Football Hall of Fame, and eight are in the Pro Football Hall of Fame. In 2009, ESPN ranked the team the third most prestigious in the country.

CHAPTER 1

A SLOW START (1890–1933)

Sports at Ohio State University (OSU) were pretty informal until 1890. In that year, George Cole talked some of his fellow students into starting a football team. He had a rulebook from the Spaulding Athletic Company and a friend who had played at Princeton. The friend, Alexander Lilley, agreed to coach. The school did not pay him, and the students had to pool their money to buy a football. In its first game, Ohio State beat Ohio Wesleyan 20–14.

Unfortunately, that win was the only victory for the new team that entire four-game season. The 1891 season started out just as poorly—with two losses. But the team managed to pull out the last two, and the school and the community began to be interested in football. The university hired its first paid coach, Jack Ryder, in 1892.

Ryder's first game was against Oberlin, which also had a first-year coach, John Heisman, for whom the most coveted trophy in college football is named. Ohio lost that game 40–0, and the team lost a second time to Oberlin 50–0. But the 1892 season had eight games instead of four, and Ohio finished with its first winning record: five wins to three losses. Enthusiasm for the sport was growing.

The team struggled in the early years, with more wins than losses in only one of the next six seasons. Interest dwindled until John Eckstorm became coach in 1899. Eckstorm led the team to its first undefeated season. That was the beginning of a long winning streak; in the twenty-three years from 1899 to 1921, Ohio had no losing season. In Eckstorm's third winning year, ticket sales for games made the football program profitable for the first time. In 1904, fifteen hundred seats had to be added to accommodate the growing crowds. Many at Ohio State felt the team was ready for the big leagues.

John Heisman, posing here when he was a University of Pennsylvania football player, coached college football for thirty-six years. The trophy named for him is given to the outstanding college player of the year.

JOINING THE BIG TEN

In its first five years, all of the university's games were against other Ohio teams. Gradually, the school scheduled contests with squads from other states. (This was probably the time the players were first called Buckeyes, a term widely applied to anyone from Ohio.) Still, most of the games in

Ohio State's first twenty-two seasons were against small local schools. When the school had racked up a string of thirteen victorious seasons in a row, its athletic board decided it was time to play more state universities. In 1912, the board asked to join the Western Athletic Conference.

By then, the conference was sixteen years old. It had begun when presidents of seven large colleges met to organize and manage the way they played various sports against one another. Other colleges joined, and when the number reached ten in 1917, the organization began to be called the Big Ten Conference. OSU's request was accepted, and the Buckeyes played their first conference game in 1913.

The first game was a disappointing one-point loss to Indiana. The second game was worse: a 12–0 shutout against Minnesota. But the Buckeyes redeemed themselves in the final conference game of the season; they pummeled Northwestern 58–0. Three of their nonconference matches were big victories—90–8 for all three—and one was a scoreless tie. The team and the fans felt good about Ohio's first year in the Big Ten.

JOHN WILCE

Much of the success was due to the new head coach, John Wilce. Wilce had graduated from Wisconsin, where he was captain of the football team for one year and assistant coach after graduation. He was only twenty-five years old when he came to Ohio. Before Wilce became coach, OSU had eleven coaches in twenty-three years. Wilce stayed for sixteen seasons, the second longest time of any coach in the school's history. Only two were losing seasons. In one game against Oberlin, the unbeaten Buckeyes scored their biggest margin of victory ever: 128–0. The young coach led the school

Script Ohio

Every Ohio State home game since 1936 begins the same way, with a tradition called Script Ohio. The school's marching band forms a triple O and unwinds it gracefully across the field to spell out the word "Ohio." A sousaphone player marches forward, bows deeply left and right, and at the close of the music stands with the instrument forming a perfect dot at the top of the "i." Fans erupt in applause and the music starts again. The audience becomes surprisingly silent and the band sings the *Buckeye Battle Cry*. Dotting the "i" is considered a great honor, and it is usually reserved for senior sousaphone players. A few famous people have been allowed the privilege, including the school's most winning coach, Woody Hayes; golf pro and Ohio State alumnus Jack Nicklaus; astronaut and Ohio State professor John Glenn; and Ohio comedian Bob Hope.

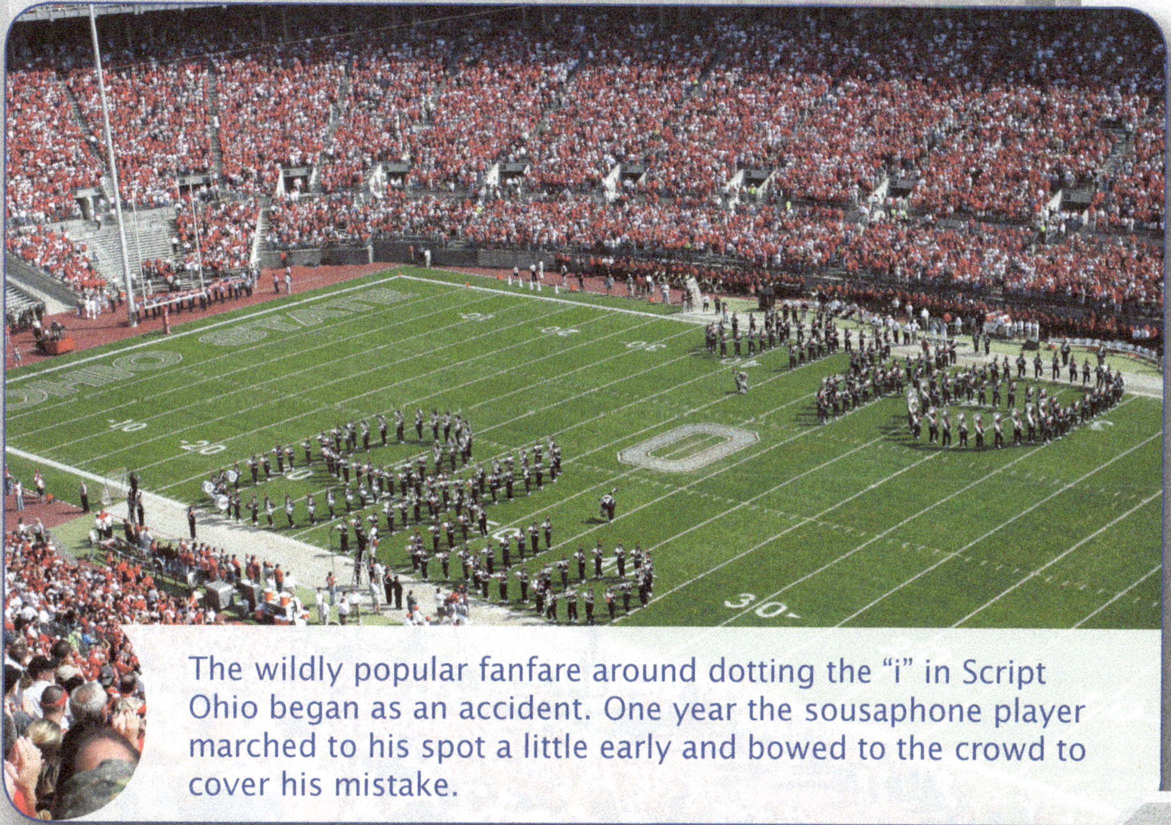

The wildly popular fanfare around dotting the "i" in Script Ohio began as an accident. One year the sousaphone player marched to his spot a little early and bowed to the crowd to cover his mistake.

to three conference championships and its first Rose Bowl game. Fourteen of his players were named all-Americans. He was still at the school in 1954, when he was inducted into the College Football Hall of Fame. Football fans all over the country began to pay attention to Ohio State.

CHIC HARLEY

John Wilce was a great coach, but it was Chic Harley who made Ohio State a great team. Harley was an all-around athlete, competing in baseball, basketball, and track, as well as football. In his three seasons as a Buckeye (1916–1917 and 1919), he played halfback, quarterback, end, kicker, punter, and safety. His very first conference game was the victory over Illinois in which Harley scored all the OSU points in the last minute and ten seconds of play.

Today, almost ninety-five years after Chick Harley played his last game at Ohio State, he still holds two school records: highest number of points per game (8.74) and most interceptions in one game (4).

The second conference game of Harley's first year was against Wilce's alma mater. Wisconsin was one of the founding members of the Big Ten and had already won four conference championships. The two teams had played each other only three times, and the Badgers had crushed the Buckeyes each time. Hopes were riding high with Harley on the team, but Wisconsin was a formidable opponent.

Harley proved up to the challenge. His first touchdown was a thrilling zigzag down the field, and his second was a spectacular 80-yard run in the last eight minutes of the game. Harley scored all 14 points in the Buckeyes' 14–13 nail-biter victory. Thousands of students mobbed the field and carried Harley off on their shoulders.

Ohio won its first Big Ten championship that year and its second the next. After missing the 1918 season to serve in World War I, Harley returned for a near-perfect 6-1 final season. He was selected all-American all three years and was the first person from OSU to be inducted into the College Football Hall of Fame. His amazing talent brought so much fame and so many fans to the school that the university needed to build a new arena. Ohio Stadium has been called "the House That Harley Built." Some call the Buckeyes "the Team That Harley Began."

CHAPTER 2

BUILDING A GREAT TEAM (1934–1950)

Football fever did not die down when Chic Harley graduated. Fans continued to pour into the new stadium, and OSU continued to win games. One thing that keeps enthusiasm for college sports high is rivalry between schools. Ohio State had two big rivals

Ohio State students raise the Illibuck trophy during their 2009 game against Illinois. The Buckeyes won the game 30–0 and got to keep the trophy for another year.

from its early days: the University of Illinois and the University of Michigan.

The Buckeyes and Illinois, opponents since 1902, became serious rivals in 1925, when the junior honorary societies of the two schools decided to add some spice to the competition. Hoping they would play each other for many years, they looked for an object that would symbolize the long life of their rivalry and that would be kept by the team that won the annual game. They settled on a live turtle. His name combined the names of the two teams: illibuck.

Unfortunately, Illibuck died two years later. The groups then bought a wooden turtle, and the tradition lives on. Today, as has been done for more than eighty years, representatives of the two honorary societies meet on the field at halftime and the trophy is presented to the team that was victorious the previous year.

RIVALRY WITH MICHIGAN

As fierce and fun as the Ohio-Illinois contest is, it fades in comparison to the century-long rivalry between the Buckeyes and the Wolverines of the University of Michigan. Although the schools had faced each other many times since 1897, the real competition began in 1935. The match was scheduled as the final game of the season for both teams. Ohio surprised Michigan, winning 38–0. From that year on, the two teams have ended almost every season by facing each other. Even after the Big Ten split the conference and placed Ohio and Michigan in different divisions, the schools still schedule themselves for a season-ending

Coach Francis Schmidt *(center)* tries to explain one of his many trick plays to his 1938 Ohio State Buckeyes. His playbook had more than three hundred plays from seven different formations.

match. They call the contest "The Game." Every year it draws a bigger audience than any other game.

One of the reasons the rivalry is so intense is that one team often spoils a great season for the other. Five times Michigan went into the final game undefeated and Ohio won; three times Michigan toppled Ohio's unbeaten record. Twenty-three times the outcome of The Game determined the winner of the Big Ten championship; sometimes it has decided who plays in the Rose Bowl and who will be the national champion. ESPN called the competition the greatest of all sports rivalries.

One of the heroes of that rivalry was coach Francis Schmidt (1934–1940). In his first four years, he shut out

GOLD PANTS CLUB

Ohio State fans were worried going into the 1934 game against Michigan. The stats for the rivalry stood at 22-6-2, with Michigan in the lead. It was Francis Schmidt's first year coaching the team, and he had only one loss so far. The Buckeyes would have had a perfect season the previous year if they had not lost to the Wolverines. Still, Schmidt was not worried. Of course we can beat them, he told people who questioned him; they put their pants on one leg at a time, just like everybody else.

Beat them they did: 34–0. That win sparked a tradition that continues today. Every year in which Ohio beats Michigan, each Buckeye player receives a gold charm in the shape of football pants engraved with his initials, the year, and the score. The winning Buckeyes become proud members of the Gold Pants Club.

Michigan all four times. His 38–0 win in 1935 remains OSU's largest margin of victory over the Wolverines.

Schmidt introduced the Buckeyes to a new kind of offense. He created at least three hundred different plays and seven different formations. The calls could be so confusing that quarterbacks carried notes about the plays inside their helmets and refreshed their memories during timeouts. Opponents never knew what to expect from the man reporters nicknamed "Mr. Razzle-Dazzle."

Schmidt's outstanding record earned him a place in the College Football Hall of Fame. In his seven years at Ohio State, he led the Buckeyes to two Big Ten championships. But one fatal flaw probably cost him his job. After four straight wins against the Wolverines, he lost to Michigan three years in a row. Ohio State was very serious about its rivalry with Michigan.

NATIONAL CHAMPIONS

After Schmidt left, Ohio became known as a graveyard of coaches. In the eight years from 1940 to 1947, the school had five different head coaches. Still, the team played great football. It won two conference championships and earned its first National Collegiate Athletic Association (NCAA) championship title.

Winning the national title in 1942 was not easy. Many of coach Paul Brown's players had enlisted in the military to fight in World War II (1939–1945), so he was left with mostly sophomores. (The NCAA did not permit freshmen to play until 1972.) Fortunately, the players who remained were outstanding. One was quarterback Les Horvath, OSU's first Heisman Trophy winner.

Another was Bill Willis, one of the first African Americans in college football. Brown coached him in track as well as football and knew his speed would make him an excellent defensive guard. Willis was named all-American in two of his three college seasons. Not only did Willis and Horvath's team win a national title in 1942 and Big Ten championships twice, but—perhaps as important—they also defeated Michigan twice.

After their time at Ohio State, both Brown and Willis went on to a new professional team, the Cleveland Browns. Both men are in the Pro Football Hall of Fame. Willis was one of the first African Americans in professional sports, joining the Browns in 1946, a year before Jackie Robinson was credited with breaking the color barrier.

THE SNOW BOWL

After winning the national championship, OSU continued to win far more games than it lost. But winning games was only one measure of success; winning against Michigan was another. The 1950 season-ender against Michigan was doubly important: the victor would claim the Big Ten conference title. As 5 inches (12.7 centimeters) of snow covered Ohio Stadium, OSU could have cancelled The Game. If the game were not played, the Buckeyes, who were ahead in the standings, would be declared conference champions. But Ohio coaches did not want to win a title by default, nor did they want to disappoint the fifty thousand fans huddled in the frozen stands. So, in a howling blizzard, the

The Snow Bowl was played in the worst blizzard in Columbus in thirty-seven years. Despite the cold, 50,503 fans came to watch the agonizing defeat.

Buckeyes and the Wolverines faced off in what has been dubbed "the Snow Bowl."

Ohio was counting on tailback Vic Janowicz, who would receive the Heisman Trophy that year and eventually be in the College Football Hall of Fame. But Janowicz had difficulty kicking the ball into 29-mile-per-hour (46.7 km/hr) winds. His one successful field goal was OSU's only score. The Wolverines did not make a single first down, but they recovered a punt in the end zone to win the game 9–3. Two weeks later, Ohio State's coach Wes Fesler resigned, ushering in one of the greatest periods in Buckeye history.

Chapter 3

A WINNING COACH (1951–1978)

Replacing Wes Fesler as head coach was not easy. OSU went through six applicants before settling on then little-known Woody Hayes. Hayes had coached two other Ohio teams and had a 33-11 record. The OSU search committee was impressed with his nineteen-game winning streak and his victory over Arizona in the Salad Bowl (now the Fiesta Bowl). But Ohio State fans were not particularly happy with Hayes's first three seasons; in 1951–1953, the Buckeyes finished fifth, third, and fourth in the Big Ten conference. One bright spot occurred in 1952: the team's first win against Michigan in nine years.

Underneath his gruffness on the field, Woody Hayes cared deeply about his players' education. He saw that they got any academic help they needed and that nearly all of them graduated.

The 1954 season was the turning point

for Hayes. The Buckeyes won all ten games, capturing the conference title, defeating USC in the Rose Bowl, and winning the national championship. Hayes went on to become one of the "winningest" coaches in college football. In his twenty-eight seasons at Ohio State, he led the Buckeyes to more victories than any other coach in the school's history: four Rose Bowl wins, thirteen Big Ten championships, and five national championships. He is in the College Football Hall of Fame.

A WINNING STYLE

Hayes made no secret of the fact that he hated to lose. He believed that winning was the result of hard work, preparation, and repetition. He worked his players hard, with very demanding practices. He prepared them by showing them tapes of their opponents' games. He drilled them on the same plays, over and over, until they got them right. Sometimes he threatened to keep them going until the lights on the practice field burned out.

Hayes did not believe in razzle-dazzle; he used only six or seven plays. He often described football as a contest of "muscle against muscle, bone upon bone, will against will." He taught his players to run and tackle. He hardly ever allowed them to throw the ball. He frequently said that only three results were possible when the ball goes in the air: a completion, an incompletion, or an interception. Two of those outcomes, he reminded his team, were not good. Hayes preferred to have his offense advance the ball little by little, forcing their way toward the end zone by brute force. His style became known as "three yards and a cloud of dust."

WHO PICKS THE NATIONAL CHAMPION?

The NCAA has no rules for deciding how a football team becomes national champion. Over the years, more than twenty different groups have tried to name the winner. The Associated Press began polling sportswriters in 1936, and others polled coaches. The different selectors used different criteria, and their results did not always agree. Titles were sometimes shared and sometimes contested. In 1998, the Bowl Championship Series (BCS) was established to clear up the confusion. The BCS combines information from polls and other sources to pick the top two teams, which play each other in a national championship game.

WINNING PLAYERS

Under Hayes, OSU produced some great college football players: three Heisman Trophy winners and fifty-six all-Americans. Hayes coached three of the five Buckeyes in the Pro Football Hall of Fame. His first big star was Howard Cassady, who played from 1952 to 1955. In his first game, he scored three touchdowns and earned the nickname "Hopalong." He seemed to hop all over the field like the popular Western movie and TV hero Hopalong Cassidy. Some have compared him to Chic Harley, saying he did for Hayes what Harley did for OSU: thrusting him into the national limelight. After graduation, the two-time all-American and Heisman winner played nine seasons of professional ball and was inducted into the College Football Hall of Fame.

In his thirty-six OSU games, Howard Cassady scored thirty-seven touchdowns. His record of most career points scored (222) held for twenty years.

The offensive lineman who cleared the way for Cassady's touchdown drives was Jim Parker, another two-time all-American. Like his OSU teammate, Parker went on to the pros, playing ten seasons with the Baltimore Colts. His spectacular blocking gave him a spot in both the College and the Pro Football Halls of Fame.

Three years after Hayes led the Buckeyes to a national championship, in 1957, he did it again. One of his best players that year was Dick LeBeau, who played both offense and defense. LeBeau spent fourteen seasons with the Detroit

Archie Griffin poses with his second Heisman Trophy in 1975. Woody Hayes called Griffin the best football player he had ever seen. ESPN ranked him among the top twenty-five players in college football history.

Lions and then coached for more than twenty years. He, too, is in the Pro Football Hall of Fame. As is Paul Warfield, a half-back at OSU and a wide receiver for the Cleveland Browns and the Miami Dolphins.

Another star player Hayes coached was Archie Griffin, three-time all-American, twice named the Big Ten's most valuable player, and the only person to win two Heismans. Griffin entered Ohio State in 1972, the first year that fresh-men were permitted on college varsity teams. He helped the Buckeyes win four conference titles and is the only person to play in four Rose Bowls. Griffin played seven seasons with the Cincinnati Bengals.

One of Hayes's most memorable squads played from 1968 through 1970. The best players on most college teams are juniors or seniors, but the 1968 team was mostly sophomores. *Sporting News* called this team, dubbed the "Super Sophs," one of the ten greatest in all of sports history. The group stayed together for three years, amassing an amazing 27-2 record. Three of the Super Sophs are in the College Football Hall of Fame: Rex Kern, Jack "the Assassin" Tatum, and Jim Stillwagon. Despite its great success, the Super Sophs had one major blot on their record: they lost to Michigan in 1969.

THE TEN-YEAR WAR

Michigan had a new coach that year: Glenn "Bo" Schembechler. Schembechler had played football for Hayes at Miami of Ohio and had served under him at OSU as assistant coach for six seasons. But that was seven years earlier, and in 1969, the two faced each other on opposite sides of a rivalry that had raged for sixty-five years.

Ohio State went into the contest the reigning champion and a seventeen-point favorite. The Buckeyes had won twenty-two straight games, including their last two against Michigan. But the Wolverines prevailed in a 24–12 upset.

Hayes managed to turn the grudge match into a war. He pounded into his players the importance of The Game and fired them up all season in preparation for it. He refused to even utter the word "Michigan," referring to the university as "that school up north." He said he hated not just the school, but everything about "that state up north."

In the ten seasons of the war, both Ohio and Michigan were powerhouses in college football. From 1969 to 1978, one or both of the two teams won the Big Ten conference; they shared the conference title six times in that period.

The war ended abruptly in 1978. That was the year Hayes's bluster became more than the OSU administrators could tolerate. Hayes was known for throwing tantrums, tossing sideline markers, and breaking things. But when he punched an opposing player for intercepting a pass during the nationally televised Gator Bowl, the university had no choice but to fire the coach that had led its team to five national championships. The fit of temper ended the twenty-eight-year career of Woody Hayes at Ohio State.

CHAPTER 4

TWO MORE WINNING DECADES (1979–2000)

Following a coaching legend would not be easy. But Woody Hayes had left his successor a strong team. That team and the squads that followed would continue Hayes's winning legacy. OSU's next two coaches would, like Hayes, perform so well that they would be inducted into the College Football Hall of Fame.

In a bittersweet moment, OSU players carry their popular coach, Earle Bruce, off the playing field on their shoulders after his last Ohio State game, a 23–20 victory over archrival Michigan.

EARLE BRUCE (1979–1987)

Earle Bruce had suffered a knee injury while a freshman, ending his hopes of playing on Hayes's varsity team. Hayes encouraged him to go into coaching, bringing him on as an assistant until he graduated and hiring him for six seasons thirteen years later. After Bruce distinguished himself at Tampa and Iowa, Ohio State brought him back as head coach to fill the shoes of his mentor.

Bruce proved himself up to the task in his first year. The Buckeyes went undefeated, winning the conference championship and a trip to the Rose Bowl. Bruce was named Coach of the Year. Ohio lost the Rose Bowl game by one point, but that loss was forgiven because of a more important achievement: Ohio beat Michigan for the first time in four years.

Bruce's remaining eight seasons were good but not spectacular. He always won more than he lost, and he took the team to bowl games in all but his last year (when he turned down an invitation to the Sun Bowl), but a national championship eluded him. Worse yet, he lost to Michigan four times. Those losses were probably the reason he was fired at the end of the 1987 season, just before The Game. With all of the players wearing headbands emblazoned with the word "Earle," Bruce's Buckeyes gave their coach a thrilling come-from-behind victory over Michigan as a parting gift.

JOHN COOPER (1988–2000)

Just as losses to Michigan may have cost some Ohio coaches their jobs, John Cooper very likely became the Buckeye coach because he beat the hated "school up north." After he led Arizona State to victory over Michigan in the 1987 Rose Bowl, Ohio State offered him the position of head football coach. However, in his thirteen years at OSU, he defeated Michigan only two times.

Despite his dismal showing against the Wolverines, Cooper coached well, with no losing seasons. In fact his 111-43-1 win-loss-tie record was the second best in Ohio

Joe Germaine looks for a receiver in the 1998 game against Michigan. Germaine went from Ohio State to St. Louis; as backup quarterback for the Rams, he earned a ring in Super Bowl XXXIV.

State history; only Woody Hayes did better. But Cooper is probably remembered more for his failures than his successes. His teams played in eleven bowl games, but they won only three.

Cooper's most exciting moment had to be the 1997 Rose Bowl. OSU had lost only one game all season—against Michigan—and was ranked fourth. The team was pitted against the number-two-ranked Arizona Sun Devils, who were undefeated. Ten years earlier, Cooper had coached Arizona State to its victory over Michigan in the Rose Bowl; this year, he was facing his old team. Adding to the drama was the fact that one of the Buckeyes' quarterbacks, Joe Germaine, had almost played for the Sun Devils. An Arizona native and Sun Devils fan, Germaine had turned down an Arizona State football scholarship and come to Ohio instead. He was a key player in the game.

In the third quarter, Germaine threw a pass that teammate Demetrious Stanley ran for 72 yards, the longest

TUNNEL OF PRIDE

In 1995, Ohio State would face Notre Dame for only the third time. Notre Dame had won the first two games, but those had been played sixty years earlier, in 1935 and 1936. The then-record crowd in Ohio Stadium was fired up. One fan who was particularly excited was Rex Kern, a College Hall of Fame quarterback who had led the Buckeyes' Super Sophs to victory in 1968–1970. He and Ohio's director of athletics, Andy Geiger, had an idea to encourage their team, let the players know how much support they had...and maybe rattle their opponents. They invited all the former Buckeyes in attendance to come on the field and form a tunnel through which the team would enter the arena. The audience cheered wildly at the visible display of connection between old and new players. After the game ended in a 45–26 win for Ohio, the Buckeyes decided to make the Tunnel of Pride a part of their most important games—the ones against the Wolverines. Ever since, the tunnel has been a feature of every Ohio-Michigan game played in the Horseshoe.

touchdown reception in OSU bowl history. It put Ohio on top 14–10, a lead that held almost to the end of the game. With less than two minutes of play left, however, Arizona scored, going ahead of the Buckeyes 17–14. Germaine had the ball again, and he moved it steadily downfield in a series of short, fast drives. Finally, in the last twenty seconds, he connected with a receiver in the end zone and Ohio won 20–17. Germaine was named Outstanding Player of the game, and Ohio State won its first Rose Bowl in twenty-three years.

GREAT PLAYERS

The OSU teams of the 1980s and 1990s were full of talent. A number of Bruce's players left Ohio State to make names for themselves in professional football, including all-Americans Keith Byars, Cris Carter, Tom Tupa, Chris Spielman, and Pepper Johnson. John Frank earned two Super Bowl rings as a San Francisco 49er, and Pepper Johnson won two Super Bowls as

Two players who eventually became consensus all-Americans battle: OSU tackle Orlando Pace *(#75)* and Penn State linebacker Brandon Short.

a New York Giant. Spielman is one of OSU's many players in the College Football Hall of Fame.

Cooper also coached some outstanding players. His 1995 squad had more awards than any other college team that year. Orlando Pace won the Lombardi Award, given to the top lineman of the year, and he won it again in 1996. Terry Glenn received the Biletnikoff Award, a trophy established the previous year for the best wide receiver. The greatest college football trophy, the Heisman, went to OSU's Eddie George. This remarkable team scored 475 points in 1995, a school record.

In the twenty-two seasons under Bruce and Cooper, Ohio State continued to win, but not as much as fans were used to. The Buckeyes won only seven conference titles, and five of those were shared with other schools. They had not had an undefeated season or captured a national championship since the days of Woody Hayes. They were ready for a change.

CHAPTER 5

STILL A WINNING TEAM

Ohio State fans were excited when Jim Tressel came to their school. He was from a coaching family. His father had coached a Division III team to a national championship and was in the

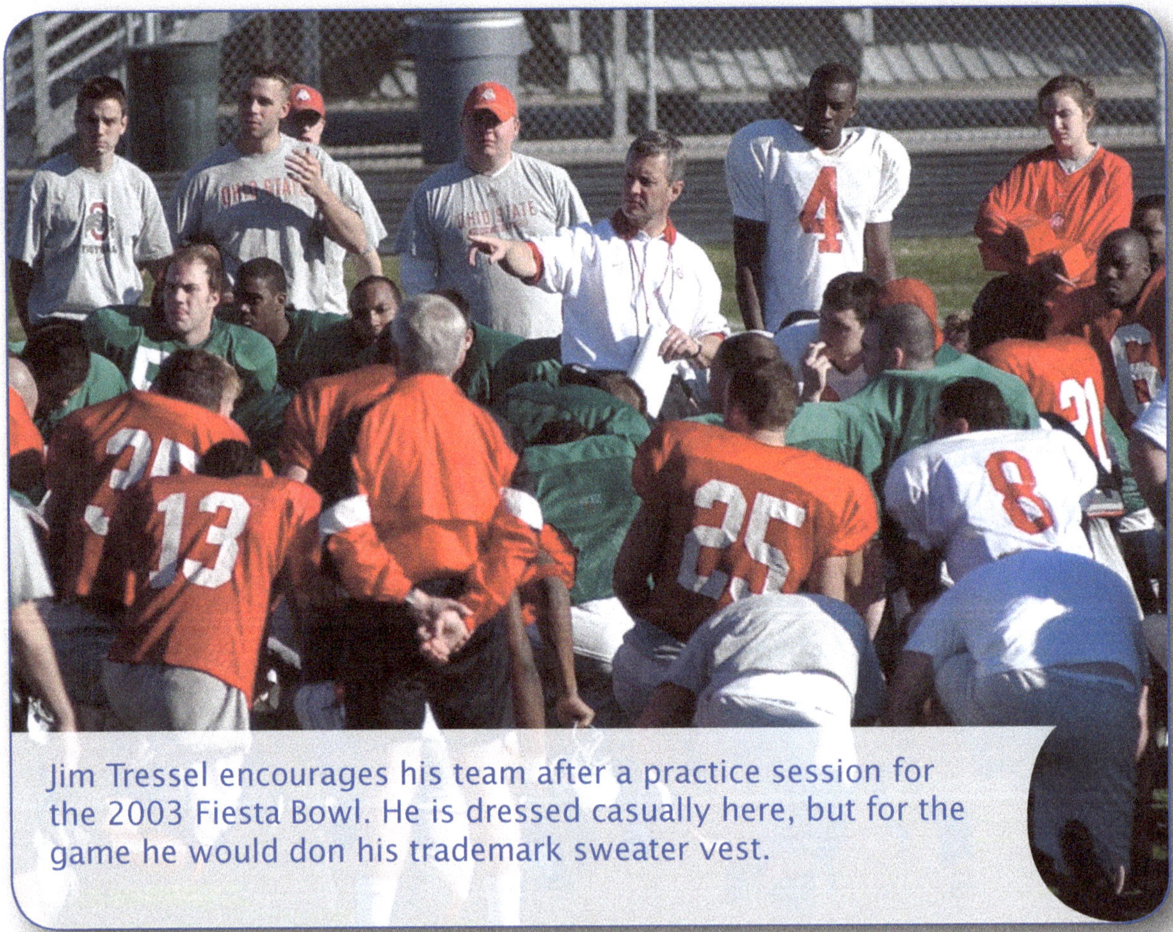

Jim Tressel encourages his team after a practice session for the 2003 Fiesta Bowl. He is dressed casually here, but for the game he would don his trademark sweater vest.

College Football Hall of Fame. His older brother was head coach at a Minnesota university. Even his mother was involved in football, working as the athletic historian of the school where her husband coached. As the young Tressel honed his own coaching skills, he served as an assistant three years under Earle Bruce. He then went to Youngstown University as head coach and compiled an impressive record there over fifteen years.

PROMISES

But Youngstown was a Division I-AA team. Could he do as well in OSU's Division I-A? Tressel thought so, and he said as much. On the day he was hired, January 18, 2001, he promised a cheering crowd at an Ohio State basketball game, "I can assure you that you will be proud of your young people in the classroom, in the community, and most especially in 310 days in Ann Arbor, Michigan, on the football field."

He began to deliver in his first year. The most important promise, of course, was to win over archrival Michigan. Ohio had succeeded in beating the Wolverines only twice in the previous thirteen years. Tressel's first season was not great—seven wins and five losses—but the coach did what really mattered. He dealt Michigan a 26–20 defeat on the Wolverines' own field. Tressel was one of only four OSU coaches to win his very first game against "the school up north."

Fans hoped for even more the next season, and they were not disappointed. Tressel's 2002 Buckeyes began the season ranked fourteenth and ended as national champions. They clinched the title at the Fiesta Bowl with a 31–24 victory in double overtime over the top-ranked Miami Hurricanes.

Jim Tressel talks with quarterback Troy Smith in 2006 before Smith led the Buckeyes to a 54–10 victory over the Northwestern Wildcats. That year Smith won seven awards in addition to the Heisman.

BREAKING RECORDS

That 14-0 season gave Ohio the record for most number of games won in a season in Division I-A football. The fourteen victories earned Tressel the American College Football Association's Coach of the Year Award. These were just the beginning of Tressel's achievements at Ohio State. From 2005 to 2009, he took the Buckeyes to conference championships all five years. No other team had ever had more than three Big Ten titles in a row. Of course, no other team had OSU Heisman winner Troy Smith either.

Tressel's successes may have been the result of a new style of playing that he introduced. It was a low-risk approach, strong on defense and very careful on offense. Its main weapon was the punt. Sportswriters dubbed the style "Tresselball," but some said it made his teams the "Luckeyes."

Tressel often won by small margins, but he did win. He enjoyed two nineteen-game winning streaks. He took the Buckeyes to a bowl game every year and won five of the nine. Even more impressive to OSU fans, he had only one loss against Michigan. His record would be even greater if it were not for a scandal in 2010 that ended his career at Ohio State.

A LOST SEASON

The NCAA has a rule that prohibits players from selling awards and team memorabilia. Some of the Buckeyes disregarded that regulation. They gave jerseys, championship rings, and other memorabilia to the owner of a tattoo parlor in exchange for tattoos, cash, and other items. When the trades were discovered, the players were suspended for several games. The suspensions, which included star quarterback Terrelle Pryor, hurt the team. An investigation revealed that Coach Tressel had known about some of the players' unlawful dealings.

Tressel had several opportunities to tell people at the school and NCAA officials about the players' violations, but he didn't. When his failure to report the players' misdeeds came to light, he was fined, suspended for five games, and eventually asked to resign (he was later allowed to retire instead of resign). The scandal cost Ohio State a great deal. The Buckeyes were prohibited from playing in any postseason competition for a year, which meant no bowl game. The team was put on probation for three years, had to give back money it had received from playing in a bowl game, and lost nine scholarships.

The university added a punishment of its own. It decided to vacate all victories for the scandalous season—that is, declare that they didn't count, as though the games had never been played. Thus the Buckeyes' twelve wins, including their defeat of Michigan, their victory in the Sugar Bowl, and their Big Ten conference title were all declared null and void. The year 2010 went down in the record books as a 0-1 season.

AFTER THE SCANDAL

One penalty for Jim Tressel's violation of NCAA rules was that, effectively, he could not coach NCAA football until the end of 2016. What would he do for five years? For a few months, he worked as a game-day consultant for the Baltimore Colts. Then he was hired by the University of Akron for a job that had nothing to do with sports.

Tressel got a big boost at The Game that ended OSU's 2012 football season. It was the tenth anniversary of Tressel's best season—the year of the Buckeyes' 14-0 national BCS championship. The 2002 team was being honored, and Tressel came to celebrate his former players. The coach was greeted with wild cheers from the crowd and a standing ovation; he was carried off the field on the shoulders of the young men he had led to victory ten years earlier.

He messed up big time, but Tressel is coming back and his future looks good.

A PROMISING FUTURE

After Tressel retired on May 30, 2011, and an interim coach finished out the year, OSU officials looked for a coach who could restore the positive momentum the school had lost. They selected Urban Meyer. Meyer was an Ohio native and had earned a master's degree in sports administration from Ohio State. He had been an assistant under Earle Bruce. He knew Ohio and he knew the Buckeyes.

He also knew how to coach. In ten seasons as head coach, he had one of the best win-loss percentages in college football history. He had won two national championships and three national Coach of the Year awards. He had retired from coaching in 2010 after six successful seasons at the University of Florida because of poor health and then

In Urban Meyer's first OSU–Michigan game, defensive lineman Nathan Williams *(center)* recovers a Michigan fumble. The Buckeyes went on to win 26–21.

worked for a year as a college football analyst for ESPN. When the offer came from OSU, Meyer was happy to return to coaching and thrilled to return to his home state.

His first game was a huge morale booster for Ohio fans—a 56–10 rout of Miami of Ohio. They needed the victory after the disgrace of 2010 and the demoralizing 2011 season. That was Ohio State's first losing season (not counting 2010) in twelve years and included a heartbreaking 34–40 loss to Michigan. Under Meyer's leadership, the Buckeyes played the 2012 season like champions even though the NCAA sanctions made the team ineligible for a Big Ten conference title and any bowl game. They ended the year undefeated, 12-0.

Playing like champions is how they had played their 122 previous seasons. It is how they won seven national titles. Playing like champions has made Ohio State one of the "winningest" teams in college football history.

TIMELINE

1890 Football begins as a varsity sport at Ohio State University.

1899 Ohio's first unbeaten season begins a twenty-three-year non-losing streak.

1913 Ohio State plays for the first time in the Western Athletic Conference (Big Ten).

1916 Coach John Wilce and Chic Harley lead Ohio State to its first Big Ten conference championship.

1919 In the schools' sixteenth match-up, Ohio State wins its first victory over University of Michigan.

1921 In its first Rose Bowl, Ohio State loses to the University of California 28–0.

1942 Ohio State wins its first NCAA national championship.

1944 Les Horvath becomes Ohio State's first Heisman Trophy winner.

1950 In its second Rose Bowl game, a repeat match against its first Rose Bowl opponent, Ohio State defeats the University of California 17–14.

1950 Vic Janowicz is named Ohio State's second Heisman Trophy winner.

1951 Woody Hayes becomes Ohio State professor of physical education and head football coach.

1954 Ohio State captures its second national championship.

1955 Howard "Hopalong" Cassady is selected Ohio State's third Heisman awardee.

1957 Ohio State wins its third national championship.

1961 Ohio State is named national champion but faculty declines Rose Bowl invitation.

1968 Ohio State wins its fifth national championship.

1969–1978 "Ten-Year War" ensues between OSU Buckeyes under Woody Hayes and Michigan Wolverines under Bo Schembechler.

1970 Ohio State captures its sixth national championship even though it lost the Rose Bowl.

1974 and **1975** Archie Griffin receives the Heisman Trophy, the only two-time winner.

1978 Woody Hayes is fired after striking Clemson middle guard Charlie Bauman during the Gator Bowl.

1979 In his first year as coach of Ohio State, Earle Bruce is named Big Ten and national Coach of the Year.

1995 Eddie George becomes Ohio State's fifth Heisman Trophy winner.

2002 Ohio State wins its seventh national championship, the first in thirty-two years.

2006 Troy Smith is named Ohio State's sixth Heisman Trophy winner.

2010 After NCAA rule violations scandal, Ohio State vacates all wins, leaving school with a 0-1 win-loss record for the season.

2012 Even though ineligible for a championship or a bowl game, Ohio State has an undefeated (12-0) season.

GLOSSARY

all-American An honor given at the end of each football season to the players who are the best at their positions. Several different groups name players to what they think would be the ideal all-America team. If three groups select the same player for a position, that player is a "consensus all-American."

alma mater The school from which a person graduated.

conference A group of teams. College Division I-A football teams are divided among twelve conferences.

division A group of teams within a conference. In any college conference, Division I teams are stronger than Division II teams, and Division II teams are stronger than Division III teams.

ESPN The company that provides sports-related programming and information in a number of media, including television, magazine, and the Internet.

halfback An offensive player who carries the ball in running plays; also called a running back or tailback.

memorabilia Objects that are valuable because they are connected to some important person or event, helping the owner to remember the person or event.

offense The players who have possession of the football and are attempting to score.

prestigious Of high status; inspiring respect or esteem.

punt A kick made by dropping the ball and kicking it as it falls. A punt is usually made on fourth down, when one team is likely to have to give possession of the ball to the other, and it is used to place the ball as far from the opposing team's goal as possible.

Rose Bowl The oldest and most prestigious annual college football game, the "Grandaddy of Them All." First played in 1902, the Rose Bowl currently pits the Big Ten and Pacific-12 conference champions against each other.

shutout A game in which the loser scores no points.

tailback An offensive player who carries the ball.

title Position of winner; championship of a particular conference or group.

USC University of Southern California, a Los Angeles school. Its football team, the Trojans, is consistently ranked among the best in its division, having won eleven national championships.

varsity The main team representing a school.

FOR MORE INFORMATION

College Football Hall of Fame
111 South St. Joseph Street
South Bend, IN 46601
(800) 440-3263
(574) 235-9999
Web site: http://www.collegefootball.org

In addition to a museum housing exhibits about college football, the College Football Hall of Fame has profiles of inductees.

National Collegiate Athletic Association (NCAA)
700 West Washington Street
Indianapolis, IN 46204
(317) 917-6222
Web site: http://www.ncaafootball.com

The National Collegiate Athletic Association manages sports competitions among college teams. In addition to setting and enforcing rules, the NCAA provides information about schedules, scores, standings, and statistics.

National Football Foundation
433 East Las Colinas Boulevard, Suite 1130
Irving, TX 75039
(972) 556-1000
Web site: http://www.footballfoundation.org

The National Football Foundation promotes amateur football by honoring those who excel and developing model football programs for youth.

Ohio State University (OSU)
281 West Lane Avenue
Columbus, OH 43210
(614) 292-6446
Web site: http://www.osu.edu

OSU is a public academic institution established in 1870, with fourteen colleges and campuses located throughout the state of Ohio.

Uplifting Athletes
P.O. Box 1298
Camp Hill, PA 17001
(717) 737-7900
Web site: http://www.upliftingathletes.org

Uplifting Athletes is a nonprofit organization in which college athletes create and implement activities that raise awareness and money and promote research and education to fight specific rare diseases. The Ohio State chapter fights Charcot-Marie Tooth Disease.

WEB SITES

Due to the changing nature of Internet links, Rosen Publishing has developed an online list of Web sites related to the subject of this book. This site is updated regularly. Please use this link to access the list:

http://www.rosenlinks.com/AMWT/OHFB

FOR FURTHER READING

Buckman, Virginia. *Football Stars*. New York, NY: Children's Press, 2007.

Danakas, John. *Choice of Colors: The Pioneering African-American Quarterbacks Who Changed the Face of Football.* Toronto, ON: Lorimer, 2008.

Deuker, Carl. *Payback Time*. New York, NY: Houghton Mifflin, 2010.

Hofstetter, Adam. *Football in the Big East Conference*. New York, NY: Rosen Publishing, 2007.

Hofstetter, Adam. *Football in the Pac-10*. New York, NY: Rosen Publishing, 2007.

Hunter, Bob. *Chic: The Extraordinary Rise of Ohio State Football and the Tragic Schoolboy Athlete Who Made It Happen.* Wilmington, OH: Orange Frazer Press, 2008.

Layden, Tim. *Blood, Sweat and Chalk: The Ultimate Football Playbook: How the Great Coaches Built Today's Game*. New York, NY: Sports Illustrated, 2010.

Morgan, David Lee, Jr. *Game Changers: The Greatest Plays in Ohio State Football History*. Chicago, IL: Triumph Books, 2010.

O'Brien, Michelle. *Historic Photos of University of Michigan Football.* Nashville, TN: Turner, 2008.

Osborne, Tom. *Beyond the Final Score: There's More to Life Than the Game*. Ventura, CA: Regal, 2009.

Porentas, John. *Glory Years: A Photo History of the New Era in Ohio State Football*. Chicago, IL: Triumph Books, 2008.

Snapp, Steve. *Diary of an Unforgettable Season: 2006 Ohio State Buckeyes*. Chicago, IL: Triumph Books, 2007.

Yuen, Kevin. *The 10 Most Intense College Football Rivalries*. New York, NY: Children's Press, 2008.

BIBLIOGRAPHY

Altvater, Fred. "Jim Tressel Receives Thunderous Applause and Standing Ovation at the Horseshoe." *Bleacher Report*, November 12, 2012. Retrieved December 5, 2012 (http://bleacherreport.com/articles/1421239-jim-tressel-receives-thunderous-applause-and-standing-ovation-at-the-horseshoe).

Beale, Joe. *The Graveyard of Coaches*. ElevenWarriors.com, November 30, 2011. Retrieved September 24, 2012 (http://www.elevenwarriors.com/2011/11/the-graveyard-of-coaches).

College Football Hall of Fame. *Earle Bruce*. Retrieved October 18, 2012 (http://www.collegefootball.org/famer_selected.php?id=80047).

College Football Hall of Fame. *John Wilce*. Retrieved September 21, 2012 (http://www.collegefootball.org/famer_selected.php?id=10041).

ESPN. *End of the Century: The 10 Greatest Rivalries*. Retrieved September 23, 2012 (http://espn.go.com/endofcentury/s/other/bestrivalries.html).

Fallica, Chris, Nick Loucks, and Harold Shelton. "Prestige Rankings: Nos. 1–5." ESPN, January 23, 2009. Retrieved September 8, 2012 (http://sports.espn.go.com/ncf/news/story?id=3849468).

Hiltbrand, Nick. "Willis Broke Through Football's Barriers." *The Lantern*, April 19, 2010.

Homan, Marv, and Paul Hornung. *Ohio State: 100 Years of Football*. Columbus, OH: Ohio State University, 1989.

Laracy, Alex. "Bowl Championship Series: 1997—Ohio State 20, Arizona State 17." ESPN, December 13, 2002. Retrieved

October 17, 2010 (http://espn.go.com/abcsports/bcs/rose/s/1997.html).

Ohio State Buckeyes Official Athletic Site. "Urban Meyer." Retrieved October 22, 2012 (http://www.ohiostatebuckeyes.com/sports/m-footbl/mtt/meyer_urban00.html).

Ohio State University. "University History and Traditions." Retrieved September 17, 2012 (http://www.osu.edu/news/history.php).

Ohio State University Marching and Athletic Bands. "Traditions." Retrieved September 16, 2012 (http://osumarchingband.com/traditions).

Park, Jack. "The Official Ohio State Football Encyclopedia". Champaign, IL: Sports Publishing, 2003.

Smith, Erick. "Ohio State Hit with Bowl Ban, Tressel Gets Show-Cause Penalty." *USA Today*, December 20, 2011. Retrieved October 21, 2012 (http://content.usatoday.com/communities/campusrivalry/post/2011/12/ohio-state-ncaa-sanctions-jim-tressel-terrelle-pryor/1#.UITa666CkZA).

Smith, Erick. "Ohio State Introduces Urban Meyer as Next Football Coach." *USA Today*, November 28, 2011. Retrieved October 22, 2012 (http://content.usatoday.com/communities/campusrivalry/post/2011/11/urban-meyer-ohio-state-coach-luke-fickell/1#.UIW3J66CkZA).

INDEX

ABOUT THE AUTHOR

Ann Byers is a writer who lives in the Central Valley of California, where the NCAA Division I California State University, Fresno, Bulldogs compete in the Mountain West Conference. She and her family are avid Bulldog fans and supporters.

PHOTO CREDITS

Cover, pp. 1, 12 Jamie Sabau/Getty Images; back cover (goal post) David Lee/Shutterstock.com; p. 4 Mike McGinnis /Getty Images; pp. 5, 14, 23, 26, 30, 32, 37 © AP Images; p. 7 Keystone Pictures USA/ZUMA Press/Newscom; p. 9 Barry Salmons/Shutterstock.com; pp. 10, 17 The Ohio State University Archives; p. 19 Tony Tomsic/Sports Illustrated /Getty Images; p. 22 TSN/Icon SMI 800/Icon SMI/Newscom; p. 28 Rick Stewart/Getty Images; p. 34 Sporting News Archive /Getty Images; multiple interior page borders and boxed text backgrounds (football) Nickola_Che/Shutterstock.com; pp. 6, 12, 19, 26, 32 (helmet) from a photo by Mike McGinnis /Getty Images; back cover and multiple interior pages background (abstract pattern) © iStockphoto.com/Che McPherson.

Designer: Nicole Russo; Editor: Kathy Kuhtz Campbell; Photo Researcher: Karen Huang